Say Anything, Anywhere, to Anyone!

Say Anything, Anywhere, to Anyone!

Table Of Contents

Foreword

Most of our problems in life come from the fact that we either agree to too much or we refuse things that we later repent. Though we may be highly educated, there is one department that most of us are lacking in... that of saying yes or no at the right place.

This e-Book delves into that collective shortcoming of the human race. If you think about it, this is quite apt. When we talk about saying anything to anyone anywhere, we are basically dabbling about the two extremities—yes and no. Either you are agreeable to what you are told, or you are not. But, it is saying it out aloud that matters.

Sometimes when you agree to too much, you might find too many things on your platter and though you have the talent to do an expert job of it, the shortage of time could be your downfall. You find that you are not able to do justice to everything that you have taken up. As a result, you lose your credibility, and people lose faith in you. Though you are an expert, your downfall was that you took up too many things. Naturally, you had to make a short shrift of things and everything did not work out as you had planned.

The other extremity could be a problem. There are some people who refuse almost anything. They have paranoia about accepting anything. Refusal is their default reaction. This could be their undoing though, because by unthinkingly refusing everything that comes in their way, they are probably losing out on a lot of opportunities. They are failing to notch up experience and goodwill. They are keeping themselves away from self-development and they are earning much negative press in the process because people usually do not like being refused something.

And then, there are times when we have a single obvious answer between yes and no, and we know that the answer we are giving out is definitely going to hurt the other person. But, we have no alternative. There is nothing we can do. What do we do in such cases?

We need to learn how to accept anything in an elegant manner. We should not take up too much and we should not take up anything that is against the principles that we have set up in life. At the same time, we should make sure that when accepting something, we are getting what we want out of it... whether it is monetary compensation or creative satisfaction or goodwill or whatever it is that is our motivation at the moment. We should also make sure that we are not coming across as too desperate when we say yes to something. Even though we may be blessed with amazing talent, if we are too desperate, then people develop a low opinion of us.

Saying no requires some special skill as well. Most importantly, we must do our best to make sure that the person we are refusing doesn't take it too hard. There should be no bitter feelings because that can create a lot of unwarranted problems in the long run. We need to justify our stance when we are refusing something. We should tell them what the reason is, and, if possible, give them an option by which they can get their job done. That usually takes care of the bad feelings part because the person whom you have just refused understands that you have not done it out of spite or because of a grudge that you have with them.

You need to learn how to strike the right balance. Between saying yes and no, there are a lot of things that you have to consider—a lot more than what you probably are considering right now—and when you eventually give your answer, you have to make it sound right.

There are times when you will have to give a quick answer. For instance, if someone you are visiting asks you to stay for dinner, you have to give a quick answer. The answer has to sound genuine and still you have to take care you are not doing anything that you do not want to do. This requires you to quickly understand the different parameters that you should think of when agreeing to or refusing something and give prompt answers that ring true.

In this eBook, we are going to speak a lot about how you can do this... say yes or no without sounding too confident or too diffident, and make sure you are not harming yourself or your near and dear ones in any way by giving your responses to the situation. You will learn how to quickly analyze a situation and give the right answer according to the situation. This is basic knowledge that everyone must have, but some people need to learn it in order to implement it in their lives.

Say Anything To Anyone - Anywhere!
Develop The Strength To Say No, The Courage To Say Yes And
The Conviction To Convince Anyone

Chapter 1:

Why We Say Yes When We Want to Say No

Synopsis

There are a lot of situations where we end up saying yes when we actually want to say no. We do such a thing and then we rue what we have done. In most cases, you cannot go back and renege on your promise. So, you are faced with a situation where you have to do something that you do not want to do, and you have to do it within a particular timeframe, which makes the issue more difficult.

So, why do we do that? Why do we end up saying yes when we should actually have refused something outright?

It is our inborn tendencies that make us do that. There are several reasons why we end up agreeing to everything that comes our way. Maybe it is the need for appreciation, or maybe it is our greed that makes us think that we can do everything that is offered to us. There are so many different reasons why this may happen, but the end result is usually always the same. It makes us feel miserable for having agreed to do what we didn't want to.

In this chapter, we shall probe into the various reasons that make us accept things as a sort of a reflex action. We shall see why it is our inherent nature to agree to things, and why refusing takes some bit of effort. We will also see how to analyze a particular request that comes our way in such a manner that we can understand whether the best answer for that would be an acceptance or a denial.

Why We Say Yes When We Want to Say No

In life, some things do not make sense. The best explanation that one can give for this is that that is how God wanted it to be. One of these things is saying yes and saying no. Most of us often find ourselves between a rock and a hard place since we find it very difficult to tell somebody no. We opt to say yes even when we are completely sure that we cannot achieve whatever it is we have promised. This can be termed as an ailment that should be dealt with immediately. The first step in dealing with it is knowing exactly why we find ourselves doing this. Here are some of the probable reasons.

Saying Yes Needs No Justification

To start with, most of us avoid giving explanations. Normally, after you say no it is only right that you try and give an explanation for doing that. Reasons such as "I will be busy" come in handy at such a time. This is exactly what most of us tend to avoid when we say yes. To some, this comes about knowingly while others just find themselves doing it unknowingly. You will find that in such cases, one says yes for the sake of saying byes but ends up messing him or herself up.

Saying Yes Creates a Positive Impression... at Least Temporarily

The other reason why saying yes is so easy unlike saying no is the urge to be liked. Deep inside, each and every one of us lies some kind of urge to be liked by those around us; it is just our nature. This urge to be liked leads us to doing some deeds that benefits others but increases stress on us. As a matter of fact, this is the main reason why saying yes tends to be easier. You can find a situation where someone has a meeting to go to in the evening, but they will miss the meeting in order to take the neighbor's child for a movie. The main reason for this is the deep urge to be liked by the neighbor. Unless we overcome this urge, saying yes will always seem far much easier as compared to doing the right thing; saying no.

We Are Too Mellow Inside

The most common reason is that most of us are too soft hearted. In that case, once someone puts in some flattery in his or her request we have no option but to foolishly follow. This is common between people of the opposite sex. Several phrases always work their magic. A good example is "no one can do it better than you" or "I do not know what I would do without you". Once someone of the opposite sex uses such phrases when asking for a favor, most of us and especially the weak at heart, say yes without even giving it a second thought. Such behavior never augers well.

There are a number of other reasons that force us into easily accepting to say yes when the correct answer is no. Overall, it is wise to stay strong and stand by what you believe. Do not be easily influenced by those around you.

Chapter 2:

When to Say Yes

Synopsis

The truth of the matter is that we agree a lot more than we should. We accept a lot more things than we can realistically fulfill. This leads to health and mental problems, and may even end up giving us a bad name in the process. When we are not able to finish the jobs that are set in front of us, we might simply not be able to tackle them all with the finesse we want to do. If you accept too many things in your line of work, then this is something that can jeopardize your prospects in an insane manner.

We need to learn when to say yes. Naturally, accepting everything is something that has to be avoided, but we cannot deny everything also. We have to take up things.

This chapter speaks about what you can say yes to within a realistic and pragmatic boundary. You should say yes to things that work for you, that are advantageous to you and that fall within the rulebook you have made for yourself in life.

Read on to know what you can say yes to, without compromising on yourself in the least manner.

When to Say Yes

Saying yes too much can end up having some pitfalls. These pitfalls will depend on the situation that the yes answer is being given. Since many situations vary, the pitfalls will also vary. One main situation that can cause someone to get some undesirable results when they say yes is when they are being offered some help. In the event that a person is in a situation that they need help, sometimes people tend to offer help. This might be because the person has so much pride such that they cannot be able to know when to ask for help.

However, when they decide to accept the help that is being offered, the person who is offering the help might decide to continue giving the help. However, they might reach a point that they get tired and decide to stop offering help. The best way to know how to say yes to somebody will be through following certain steps. The steps will have to be followed in order for one to know the right time to say yes and the right time to say no.

The first thing that should be done is an evaluation of the reason why they have to make a decision. You might find that a person will want some financial help from you. When this happens, you can decide to agree or to disagree. You can agree by looking at the situation in a thorough manner. The first thing that you should ask yourself is if you are able to offer the help that is needed. For example, if someone wants a certain amount of money and you have it, you can easily say yes. But before you say yes, you should look at the person who is asking you for the money. They may be an addict and therefore will use the money for the wrong reasons. If this is the case, you should avoid giving them money.

Secondly, the person might be having an emergency. This might be medical or otherwise. In such a situation, you can squeeze yourself and see if you can agree to give them some money. Make sure that they understand that the money was to be used in a certain way so that they pay you back as soon as possible.

Thirdly, you should make sure that you are not going to be inconvenienced when you agree to something. There are some people who are too generous and they agree to things that will inconvenience them. They may not realize it but the inconvenience might lead to other negative results. To avoid such a situation, a person should make sure that they will be comfortable when they agree to do something for someone.

Making sure that you do not inconvenience yourself is a great way to make sure that you have a long and productive life. When one follows such guidelines, they will avoid a lot of stress in their life. They will have smooth relationships and they will also succeed in most of the things that they do. This is one of the secrets of successful people.

Chapter 3:

When to Say No

Synopsis

There are times when we have to say no. We have no option, and we have to refuse the opportunities that come along our way. But, we have to understand when we cannot do everything, of course, and hence refusal becomes an important weapon that we have to use sometimes.

But, when we are refusing something, we are already treading a very delicate line. Nobody likes to hear a refusal. If we are saying no to something, taking care that we do not end up offending them is a very important thing we have to do. We have to justify our reasons when we are doing so.

To cut a long story short, saying no isn't something that we can do just like that. We have to give it a thought and only when we are seriously not able to do something should we refuse it.

In this chapter, we see about the situations in which we can say no, and it would be justified.

When to Say No

In life, some things are better off when they are left alone. This is why it is very important for each and every one to learn how to say no to things that will not bring any kind of benefit to his or her life. Most of us find it very difficult to do this. This can be attributed to the fact that many people tend to follow the will of others all in a bid to make them like you. However, this is not necessary. In fact, by saying yes to everything other people say, then you end up saying no to yourself. In addition, this is not healthy.

Overall, use the word no wisely. Do not just use it anyhow. At times, it might sound rude depending on the situation it has been used. Here are some cases when the word no is to be used.

1. *When the favor is beyond your might*

   At times, people tend to ask for favors that are extreme. But since we have this urge to be liked, especially with persons of the opposite sex, we find ourselves saying yes. In the end, we get inconvenienced and at times we do not even fulfill whatever it is we had promised to do. Actually, the other party eventually gets annoyed with you. It is therefore wise to say no in such cases. A good example is if someone tells you to do his or her shopping for her whereas you know that your day's schedule is quite tight. Why not just say no in a good way instead of disappointing him or her!

2. *If it violates your principles*

I am sure that everyone has some set principles that help them live their day to day lives in an upright manner. Though the principles might be different in terms of character, they still are principles and it is your duty to ensure you never violate them. A good example of a principle is to never have sex with a stranger. Many have this in their list of principles. If you are one of them, it is up to you to learn how to say no when you come across someone that expects you to do it with them and you barely even know him or her. No matter the situation, stand by your word!

3. *If your instincts tell you to say no*

Have you ever found yourself avoiding a particular route home in the evening just because you have this bad feeling? This is known as the sixth sense. God created us all with this sense for a reason. It acts as our danger detectors. It tends to warn us when something is not going well. In that case, if the sixth sense tells you not to agree to something please do just that. There are cases when people are conned or robbed just because of not listening to their sixth sense. In short, always say no if it does not feel right.

Generally, learn to say no or you will put yourself in great jeopardy saying yes to everything!

Chapter 4:

The Dangers of Saying Yes Too Much

Synopsis

Quite unknowingly, we often end up saying yes to more things than we can handle. We do not know how this can seriously affect several things that we stand for, including our impression in society and our health.

In this chapter, we will see how saying yes to too many people and too many requests could actually backfire. We may be well meaning about it, we may want to do something to earn more money or do something just because we want to do a favor on our near and dear ones, but if we have too many things on our platter, the danger is that we might not be able to accomplish them all and that is when the problems begin to emerge.

Saying yes to too many things is never an option. You have to be sure about what you are doing. Here we see what the dangers of agreeing to too many things can be, and how sticky situations can be avoided.

The Dangers of Saying Yes Too Much

Remember the good old days when we used to attend Sunday school? The pastor always told us to ensure we be good to each and every person we met throughout the week. Back then, this was quite convenient. Today, it seems illogical. The same applies to saying yes, since it also entails being good. I might sound silly but it is true; Saying yes to everyone is dangerous. To prove this theory, let us take a look at some dangers that are associated with saying yes excessively.

Denying Yourself

To start with, saying yes to everyone is the same as saying no to yourself. Usually, you are denying yourself several things by agreeing to something that someone else says. At times, we say yes to favors that are way beyond our might. Therefore, we end up stressing our resources all in a bid to please whomever it is that asked for the favor. We sacrifice our comfort for others, and in most cases, the other party is of the opposite sex. This not worth it since it never ends up well.

We always end up fatigued and without having fulfilled the promise we had made. As a result, the other person gets angry with us. I am sure that this is the last thing you had in mind when saying yes. Therefore, be sincere and say "no, I cannot" instead of risking whatever the kind of relationship you had with the other party.

Increasing Your Vulnerability

Secondly, saying yes excessively increases your vulnerability. You will be the key target for many predators. In this case, predators refer to the like of conmen or even thieves.

Recent research shows that about sixty percent of conning and kidnapping situations have been aided by the good will of the victim.

A good example is a situation whereby a stranger asks for a lift in your vehicle at the middle of the night. For safety precautions, it is advisable to say no. Nevertheless, since some of you cannot say no, they end up getting hurt. I have heard of cases whereby people get conned out of their property just because they did not say no while some got robbed just because they did not say no to strangers entering their houses. To be on the safe side, learn how to say no especially when it comes to dealing with strangers.

Submission to Others

In addition to this, saying yes excessively may turn you into a servant unknowingly. This might sound illogical but it is true. Sorry to say, but am sure some of you are already victims of this. Picture a situation where a particular neighbor always asks you to do their shopping for them every weekend. This is because you always said yes ever since the first time he or she asked you. Ever since then, they always have a reason why they cannot do their shopping themselves and you end up doing it on their behalf.

Have you ever sat down and asked yourself why they chose you out of the rest of the neighbors? The answer is because know your weakness; you can never say no! I am not telling to become mean, but be wise.

It is good to be good, but limit it!

Chapter 5:

The Pitfalls of Saying No Too Much

Synopsis

Just as agreeing to everything that comes your way can be a problem, declining everything can be a problem as well. in fact in this case, the difficulties are more profound. Since no one wants to take no for an answer, this can lead to several delicate situations.

It is for this reason that you have to be completely sure when you are rejecting something. You have to be absolutely certain that this is something you do not want to do or cannot do and that is the reason you are refusing it. There should be no ulterior motives.

However, there may be situations when you cannot justify your refusal to someone. This could lead you to a tight spot and you would definitely not want to be in a soup. But, it you are certain about your reason, then you can go ahead and take the step of refusing the thing that you do not want to do.

At the same time, remember that saying no without reason can have a lot of negative consequences for you. Least of all, you might miss out on a great opportunity. Every opportunity presents itself quite innocuously at first, and you have the choice to accept it or reject it. If you reject everything that comes your way, you may not be sure what you are saying no to. Also, this may become a habit. If you start saying no to everything habitually, then it can garner a negative impression for you. You have to be careful about such things. In this chapter, we shall see about the various pitfalls in saying no to someone.

The Pitfalls of Saying No Too Much

Saying no is one of the hardest things to do for some of us. Most of us tend to say yes blindly to every little thing people ask us to do and this never ends up well. However, there are those that have mastered the art of saying no. Such people are those that are strong at heart and are not easily swayed by what other people think of them. They live their own private lives and do not appreciate people who try to poke their noses in their business. This lifestyle tends to have its own pros and cons. Here are some of its cons.

Avoid the Habit of Refusing

Saying no too much over a long period of time tends to grow in you as a habit and eventually leads to a mean mentality. This mentality will gradually grow in you since you it will not be a big deal to say no. Once this mentality fully grows in you, others will even stop asking for favors from you since they are sure you will just say know. In addition, this is risky! Remember, no man is an island. A time will come when you will need some kind help from others and at such a time, you will suffer alone. This is the same as dying a lonely death.

Lost Opportunities?

On top of this, you will miss a lot of opportunities that might help in the future. For example, once someone asks you to help him or her run her business for a day and you say no. This is a whole truck load of opportunities that you may have benefited from. To start with, you might have earned a couple of dollars by helping the individual. And even though you do not need the cash, there is still a lot that you would have learnt in that short time. Maybe, whatever you would have learnt might come in handy one time or the other. Therefore, think twice before you say no. You might be letting go of a gracious opportunity.

Marring Relationships with Others

On the other hand, saying no frequently may lead to poor relations between you and those around you. This comes about because of the poor manner in which you relate and socialize with them. There is no way in earth that you can say no to everything someone asks you and you still end up friends. This is next to impossible. In short, saying no excessively might deny you most of your friends.

Against the Human Grain

Generally, saying no exceptionally defies the essence of humanity. Humanity entails the manner in which people live together as one. Human beings should help each other out and care for the welfare of their neighbors. This way, some sort of cohesiveness can exist between human beings and as a result; peace will reign.

Therefore, when one goes against this and begins saying no to everyone's wish, the essence of humanity is lost. Overall, I never said that you should never use the word no. Just use where necessary!

Chapter 6:

Synopsis

We become better people if we can strike the right balance between saying yes and saying no. We should know when to let go and when to draw a line. As we have seen in previous chapters, both saying yes too much and saying no too much can spell problems for us.

When we want to develop the confidence of saying anything to anyone anywhere, we have to be sure that we can say yes or no in the right measure.

Most times, it is thinking about the repercussions that helps us along our way. When we know what our actions can bring, we are prepared to handle situations and we gear ourselves up for them.

We are also able to act in such a way that we can please the greatest number of people at any given time. We cannot please everybody, but we should at least make sure that we are able to do things for the greatest good.

Striking the Balance between Saying Yes and Saying No

A few things determine choosing a negative or positive response. The first thing that will come in mind is the type of situation that requires an answer. In order to have a good balance of the two answers, you should look at several factors. These factors will determine whether you respond positively or negatively. To know these situations, you should evaluate them in a certain way.

The first things that you should consider is the type of question that you have been asked. The question can be a request for something to be done.

> *For example, when someone is broke and they are asking you for money, you should be careful how you respond to their request. If you have money and you can spare some of it, you can agree to their request. However, if you do not have any money, you should respond negatively. Even in the event that you have some little money, the negative answer should be used.*

This way, you will not find yourself without enough money for your use. At the same time, the person who is asking you for the money sold also be taken into consideration. If it is a person who you can trust, you should answer positively as long as you have some money to spare. If it is a person who you are unsure of, you can answer negatively in order to avoid future complications.

However, if it is someone who is always asking for help and does not normally refund the money, you should answer negatively most of the time. This will prevent them from coming back to you when they have such a situation. In some cases, you will find that someone is requesting for your expertise on something.

> *For example, if you are a technician, the person might need your experience in solving a problem. This can be given freely for the first time. If the person insist on calling you every time they encounter a problem, you should make sure that you answer negatively most of these times. This should be the case when the person is in need of your services and they do not pay for the same. However, if a person is paying for the services, you should make sure that you answer positively.*

Giving a positive answer will ensure that you get the work that was being given. Having this knowledge is very important in maintain a balance between saying yes and no. Without this balance, you might end up having many things going astray. You will need to have a system where you are able to do your things according to your program. This way, one will easily be successful in life. People who are successful will never have a problem deciding when to say yes or no.

Having this characteristic is the one thing that has made them successful. In the event that you do not follow this procedure, you will end committing yourself to things that you will not be able to achieve. Balancing your yes and no answers is one of the main keys to success.

Chapter 7:

Agreeing Elegantly—
Ensuring You Don't Come Across as Too Desperate

Synopsis

When you are saying yes to something, there are a few things that you have to keep in mind. You do not have to sound too eager in most situations, because this will end up in some serious situations that you won't be able to wrangle out of, such as more similar requests coming your way in future. Also, people may develop a low opinion of you when you behave in a too eager fashion for anything that comes you way.

There are some rules that you have to follow. You have to be elegant about it. At the same time, you have to ensure that you are not doing anything that you do not want to do, because this will make you lose your motivation soon and you will not be able to finish what you have taken up.

In this chapter, we will see what those rules are for saying yes to somebody without feeling too desperate about it. This is a talent that can take you places!

Agreeing Elegantly—
Ensuring You Don't Come Across as Too Desperate

Life can be very tricky if a person does not know how to live it carefully. By living careful, what is supposed to happen is that on should know when to say yes and no. At the same time, they should agree in a manner that will not put them across as being desperate. Agreeing in such a manner can be an easy or hard task depending on the person's outlook of things. In some cases, a person might be too eager to agree to something. This eagerness might be interpreted to be desperation. In some cases, this desperation might lead to the other person taking advantage of the situation.

In order to avoid such a scenario, one has to know how to control their eagerness when they are being offered something.

> *For example, you might be in the service industry. Someone might want to give you a job in your field. If you agree too enthusiastically, the might decide to reduce the amount of money that they are supposed to pay you. This reduction will lead to unsatisfactory compensation on your part. To avoid all this, you can practice some things that will make sure you do no end up in the same situation.*

The first thing to do is to digest what is being said. If a person or an organization offers you a job, you should first realize the magnitude of what is being offered. Sometimes, one might assume that what is being offered is something they can do easily. This is the case when a person evaluates something on a face level basis. However, after careful consideration, you will find that the quotation you will be giving from the top of your head might be too low. The best way to avoid such a situation would be to agree to something after thinking it out clearly. You can request the person to give you some time to think about it. This way, you will have the chance to thoroughly evaluate the situation.

After thorough evaluation, some things will come to mind. One of the things that you will discover is the amount of time that is required to handle the task. This will make you plan your time in accordance to the requirements of the situation. Lacking this time factor when you agree to something will lead to poor time management. You might end up having problems with time management and handling the task within the stipulated time.

Agreeing elegantly might be the best decision you ever make. There are several ways that you can go about it. When someone offers something, you can answer saying that you are grateful for the offer but you have to sit on it for a while. They will probably understand your reasons and give you a period.

You can also suggest that you have some details discussed before you make a decision. These details will vary according to the offer that is being made. This way, when you agree, you will have given a perception that you are not in a desperate situation.

Chapter 8:

Refusing Politely—
Ensuring There Are No Hurt Feelings

Synopsis

Refusals should never be too hard. If you have to say no to somebody, you have to be very cautious about it. Definitely this is something that people do not take lightly. Who likes to be refused?

However, there are some ways in which you can go about your refusals and still make sure that no one is hurt.

There are some common rules that apply to all types of situations where you are refusing someone. These guidelines will help you make elegant refusals that work sound acceptable and you do not lose out on your credibility or make enemies in the process.

In this chapter, we see those rules of refusal. We learn how we can refuse in a polite manner so that it is not taken too hard. In the kind of times that we live, it is very important to learn these techniques so that we do not generate too much ill will in the process.

Refusing Politely—
Ensuring There Are No Hurt Feelings

Rejecting an offer for something has to be done in a way that will ensure the other party will not feel rejected. Doing it this way helps a person understand the reasons for your negative answer.

For example, if a person offers you a cup of tea, there are two ways that you can answer negatively.

In the first method, you will answer no and leave it at that. Using this method is not advised. This is because the other party might take the rejection personal. They might think you rejected them because of something else. This might not be the case but the other party will not be able to understand you did not have any bad intentions. They might think that you do not want to have tea in their place.

The second method is by refusing politely and giving your reasons. It is not mandatory to explain yourself, but it is advisable. You can decline taking the tea by saying no thanks. You can further explain that you had just eaten or you have an issue with tea. You can further tell them that you can have coffee instead. By doing this, the other party will have a full understanding of your reasons for rejecting an offer. They will not have reasons to think that you have other intentions nor will they have hurt feelings.

The same case will apply in business. A person might offer you a job or a business venture. In this situation, it might be taken as pride when you reject an offer plainly. However, you can explain to them that your plate is full at the moment and you cannot embark on anything else. You can even assure them that once you are through with what you are doing, you will be ready and willing to work on what they wanted you to work on. Be sure to be thankful for the thought and/or suggestion that they have made.

Most of the business relationships that have gone sour do so because of slight misunderstandings. Someone might think that you are not respecting them and that is why you have refused their offer. They might even think that you do not consider them as worthy people to do business. This might bring a lot of hurt feelings to the rejected party. The might even start planning how they can destroy you and your business. Sometimes, the results have turned to be fatal.

Relationships are the most sensitive areas for rejection. When someone wants to go out on a date with you and you refuse, it might lead to hurt feelings. If you are not able to come up with a good excuse, you can tell them that you appreciate the offer but you are already seeing someone. When you tell them this, they will not take the negative answer personally. They will understand that you are committed to someone and if it were not the case, you would have gone out with them. Having such things in mind will help you be able to get what you want without stepping on anybody's toes.

Wrapping Up

We cannot do without interacting with several people each day, unless we are stranded on an island or something. We need to talk with people; we are social beings after all. We are sharing ideas, talks and things. We are each other's support a lot of times and actually, it won't be wrong to say that every individual's progress is pegged on how people around them react to them.

Essentially, this is what brings a lot of requests to us each day. In fact, it will be right to say that almost everything that is said to us is a request in some form or the other. And, everything that we say is a response to that request.

We have two options that it all boils down to. We can either say yes to the request that is placed before us, or we can say no to it. There are just these two options. Like a burning bit of plastic that leaves just a speck behind, if we are able to burn all our conversations with people, the speck that will be left behind will be this... whether we say yes or no to it.

That is why, when we wrote this e-Book, we understood that we have to actually write about how people can effectively say yes or no to others. This has to be done in a most convincing manner. Whether you are accepting or refusing something, you have to be genuine and sincere about it. You have to make sure you are not rubbing anyone the wrong way. That is simply not done.

That is the purpose of this e-Book—to tell you how you can speak with anyone in a convincing manner. Essentially, that mean how you can say yes or no to anyone in a convincing manner.

Hopefully, this e-Book has helped you in its objective. Hopefully, now you know how you can say yes or no to someone and really mean it.

All the best in your life!!!